NUGGETS OF LIFE
Over 200 Nuggets of Wisdom for Everyday Living

by
Dave Meyer

Harrison House
Tulsa, Oklahoma

Unless otherwise indicated, all Scripture quotations are taken from The Amplified Bible. Old Testament copyright © 1965, 1987 by Zondervan Corporation, Grand Rapids, Michigan. New Testament copyright © 1958, 1987 by the Lockman Foundation, La Habra, California. Used by Permission.

4th Printing

Nuggets of Life —
Over 200 Nuggets of Wisdom for Everyday Living
ISBN 0-89274-974-1
(Formerly *Dave's Nuggets,* ISBN 0-944834-07-8)
Copyright © 1996 by Dave Meyer
Life In The Word, Inc.
P. O. Box 655
Fenton, Missouri 63026

Published by Harrison House, Inc.
P. O. Box 35035
Tulsa, Oklahoma 74153

Printed in the United States of America. All rights reserved under International Copyright Law. Contents and/or cover may not be reproduced in whole or in part in any form without the express written consent of the Publisher.

Introduction

A man of understanding sets skillful and godly Wisdom before his face . . . .
Proverbs 17:24

For a number of years, friends and partners of Life In The Word, Inc./Joyce Meyer Ministries requested that we compile Dave's growing collection of "nuggets" into a book.

Those "nuggets," dictated by the Holy Spirit, are contained in this book. We urge you to incorporate them into your daily devotions. Once you have finished the book, start all over again, then again! Let these "words of wisdom" sink down deep on the inside of you.

Our prayer is that you will find the encouragement and advice you need to discover God's practical guidance for your life.

God wants you to know that if you will do what you can do, He will do what you can't do.

The Lord God is my Strength, my personal bravery, and my invincible army; He makes my feet like hinds' feet and will make me to walk [not to stand still in terror, but to walk] and make [spiritual] progress upon my high places [of trouble, suffering, or responsibility]!

Habakkuk 3:19

A position of power can be obtained in a Christian's life when he has learned to be encouraged in a discouraging situation.

Are you living on the ragged edge
or the cutting edge?

Visions never start with completion;
they do start with commitment.

Extended inactivity is disguised procrastination.

Obedience delayed is disobedience!

Your mouth is the doorway to the expression of your soul.

For the Word that God speaks is alive and full of power [making it active, operative, energizing, and effective]; it is sharper than any two-edged sword, penetrating to the dividing line of the breath of life (soul) and [the immortal] spirit, and of joints and marrow [of the deepest parts of our nature], exposing and sifting and analyzing and judging the very thoughts and purposes of the heart.

Hebrews 4:12

By your words, are you prophesying the devil's doom, or is the devil dooming your prophecy by closing your mouth?

Failure or victory is conceived in our thinking
first then birthed in our lives.

An attitude is a way of life formed by negative
or positive decisions made in the midst of circumstances
we are experiencing or have experienced.

The life you lead now may be the result of the attitude you had in the past, and the attitude you have of the future can be the result of the life you lead now. (This can become a trap.)

The Word teaches us to put the best construction on every thing. Your future is determined by what it is constructed of — what you say or do under pressure.

When the pressure is on, it is the most important time for you to press through.

If you consider your problem, how can you remember the Lord? Focus on Him, then He can deal with the problem.

All Christians love growth in the spirit,
but many don't love growing. Remember the
formula for growth is a period of growing.

It's uncomfortable for the flesh to be crucified.
It's uncomfortable for the spirit if it's not crucified.

God does not give us overcoming life; He gives us life as we overcome.

If you don't spend time with the Lord,
you won't spend time for the Lord.

Some say not to be so heavenly minded that
you're no earthly good. Yet many are so earthly
minded that they are no heavenly good.

Many times Christians want God to give them peace in the midst of what they want to do, even though they know what God has told them to do.

Conviction is meant to convince you — not to condemn you.

Guard and keep [with the greatest care] the precious and
excellently adapted [Truth] which has been entrusted [to you],
by the [help of the] Holy Spirit Who makes His home in us.
2 Timothy 1:14

When you sin, take responsibility for your action, but don't take responsibility for your restoration. That's God's job!

God formed us. Satan deformed us. Christ transformed us.

Having a weakness is not a problem.
The problem is having it and not knowing you do.

Anytime God convicts you in a situation,
His grace is then available to restore you in the same.

Jesus will be Savior without your behavior.
If you've allowed Him to be Savior,
He'll change your behavior.

Our obedience to and our appreciation for increase
is dependent upon our perception of God's Word.

If you live in the prosperity of tomorrow today,
you may live in poverty tomorrow.

Learn to plant seed in the hard times,
and you will hardly notice them.

If you will be a blessing when you're hurting,
you will be planting seeds to be blessed in future hurts.

God knew what you would be before you became, because He saw who you were while you were still becoming.

Faithful is He Who is calling you [to Himself] and utterly trustworthy, and He will also do it [fulfill His call by hallowing and keeping you].
1 Thessalonians 5:24

God's waiting for you. Come as you are,
not as you're trying to become.
He'll make you what you are to be.

Be the best! Who you are, you can be.

If I believe I should be blessed more
than I am, it may be because my head
has become bigger than my heart.

Pride brings trouble which
God uses to pop your bubble.

Fame without humility is fatal.

God will honor you if you go beyond your feelings to obey Him.

❦   ❦   ❦   ❦   ❦   ❦   ❦

Blessed (happy, fortunate, and to be envied) is the man who reverently and worshipfully fears [the Lord] at all times [regardless of circumstances], but he who hardens his heart will fall into calamity.

Proverbs 28:14

While you are waiting to get where you are going, you must learn to enjoy where you are.

We have no right to steal God's glory —
His glory is a result of His grace.

Works are a waste if not done by grace.

If you put your schedule before God, the devil will make sure He doesn't have a place. If you work your schedule around God, everything else will fall into place.

Prayer is the exercise of drawing
on the grace of God.

To receive the grace of God,
we must stop trying to get it.

God's grace is His power at work in and around you to keep you until you change, to bring you to the threshold of change and to change you.

For God's child, God's grace will cover any negative situation, but it will not cover the fear of a future negative situation.

The fear of the Lord is to know God as a just God.

The reverent, worshipful fear of the Lord leads to life,
and he who has it rests satisfied;
he cannot be visited with [actual] evil.
Proverbs 19:23

There is no rest until you pass the test prepared by the pest.

The authenticity of a person is seen when his exterior truly reflects his interior.

Deception is a result of exalting our opinion above the Word of God.

The great test of every Christian
is not preaching what he's learned,
but living what he preaches.

In true faith, the proof is not in the profession, but in the procession.

For in the Gospel a righteousness which God ascribes is revealed, both springing from faith and leading to faith [disclosed through the way of faith that arouses to more faith]. As it is written, The man who through faith is just and upright shall live and shall live by faith.

Romans 1:17

Are you impressed by your circumstances
or by the Word of God? Whichever
you choose determines whether
you walk in faith or in fear.

True faith is timeless. It can only be interrupted by two things — doubt or manifestation.

Faith in God is hope at rest.

Are you planning to succeed,
or are you planning to avoid failure?
These two statements are worlds apart.
The first is positive and done in faith; the
second is negative and operates in fear.

Christians must learn to be excited when they are believing, not just when they are receiving.

To receive, a believer must believe instead of achieve.

The manifestation of great faith is to trust God without having received any indication of what you're believing God for.

If the Word of God has been hidden in your heart, it will draw on the grace of God in times of trouble.

My son, attend to my words; consent and submit to my sayings. Let them not depart from your sight; keep them in the center of your heart. For they are life to those who find them, healing and health to all their flesh.

Proverbs 4:20-22

It is entirely possible for God to sovereignly heal someone at the same time that I pray for them, not because of my faith, but to prove whether I'm humbly grateful or proudly boastful of his or her healing.

If your heart is hidden in God,
your life will be exposed to the world.

Our worth is not found in our works,
but in His finished work.

Tomorrow may not come, and yesterday is past. We must live each day as though it is our last.

If you will trust God as your Source, He will trust you with His Resource.

But you shall [earnestly] remember the Lord your God, for it is He Who gives you power to get wealth, that He may establish His covenant which He swore to your fathers, as it is this day.

Deuteronomy 8:18

Farmers have formulas for planting, but not for reaping. Planting is in our hands, and reaping is in God's hands.

Fear of giving hinders our freedom of living.

Don't be so busy trying to keep what God has given you that you miss what God is trying to give you.

Don't be afraid of losing what you have; for if you are, you've already lost the enjoyment of having it.

If your offering doesn't touch you,
it won't touch God.

The limits of gifts are established by God.
The limits of giving are established by man.

Give in secret. If you are to receive a reward, you cannot blow your own trumpet. Whoever blows his trumpet, blows his reward.

If you will not run when you feel fear, fear will run because it has seen faith.

And do not [for a moment] be frightened or intimidated
in anything by your opponents and adversaries, for such
[constancy and fearlessness] will be a clear sign (proof and seal)
to them of [their impending] destruction, but [a sure token and
evidence] of your deliverance and salvation, and that from God.
Philippians 1:28

Does opposition stir you up or shut you up?

Don't be afraid of the darkness in the Earth today.
Remember this: light shines best in darkness.

You can never be a "lesser than" unless you are intimidated by someone you think is a "more than."

You can't be excluded if you don't need to be included.

If you are spending much time wondering what's wrong with you, you are purchasing a bad attitude.

Usually the first thing on your heart is the last thing on your mind.

Delight yourself also in the Lord, and He will give you the desires and secret petitions of your heart.

Psalm 37:4

God wants to make His interests
your interests, not your interests
His interests, unless your interests
have become His interests.

We need to learn to live by the presence of the Lord, not by the presents of the Lord.

Many people do not fully enjoy their friends because they covet their gifts.

We'll never receive any of God's blessings for ourselves if we don't spend any of our time with God.

If God prompts us to do good and we disobey, He is never disappointed in us — but for us.

[What, what would have become of me] had I not believed that I would see the Lord's goodness in the land of the living!
Psalm 27:13

God's manifest presence with us is a result of our manifest presence with Him.

Your flesh can't keep you happy, so why don't you stop trying to keep it happy. Obey the Spirit, and the desires of the flesh will die.

I have been crucified with Christ [in Him I have shared His crucifixion]; it is no longer I who live, but Christ (the Messiah) lives in me; and the life I now live in the body I live by faith in (by adherence to and reliance on and complete trust in) the Son of God, Who loved me and gave Himself up for me.

Galatians 2:20

It is hard to die to the flesh,
but it is harder to live in the flesh.

Works of the flesh seek man's credit;
works of the spirit give God credit.

If Jesus is going to live in you,
He is going to live on His terms, not yours.

Self must be nailed for God to be hailed.

Death to the flesh equals willingness
to hurt until hope is fulfilled.

The flesh has no balance;
it either wants to do nothing or everything.

Growing up spiritually is painful to the flesh but freedom to the spirit. Remaining a child spiritually is painful to the spirit but freedom to our flesh. In each case, there is pain. One is pain to death; the other is pain unto life.

The more God's going to do with you, the more He's got to deal with you.

For the time being no discipline brings joy, but seems grievous and painful; but afterwards it yields a peaceable fruit of righteousness to those who have been trained by it [a harvest of fruit which consists in righteousness — in conformity to God's will in purpose, thought, and action, resulting in right living and right standing with God].

Hebrews 12:11

The cutting edge of God in our lives can become dull if we resist His chastening love.

Love without truth is permissiveness.

If you're soft on sin, you cannot
be tender toward God.

God will do whatever is required to draw the impurities out of you and get you to face them so that He can deal with them and you can go free.

The devil likes to set you up to be upset.

And the servant of the Lord must not be quarrelsome (fighting and contending). Instead, he must be kindly to everyone and mild-tempered [preserving the bond of peace]; he must be a skilled and suitable teacher, patient and forbearing and willing to suffer wrong. He must correct his opponents with courtesy and gentleness, in the hope that God may grant that they will repent and come to know the Truth [that they will perceive and recognize and become accurately acquainted with and acknowledge it].

2 Timothy 2:24,25

Pressure without relief becomes a destructive force. Our attitude is our relief valve.

Deal with situations. Anything that you
hide from will eventually find you.

It's easy to give people what they deserve,
but it's a privilege to give them mercy.

If you are waiting for God to change someone, don't forget to enjoy your life while you are waiting.

Are you in competition with other people
or in compassion for other people?

Attitude is the determining factor between
being blessed or being miserable.

Many people who have been hurt spend their whole lives paying back or collecting debts. This is God's job — not ours. He's our vindicator and our recompense.

Excuses are dangerous because they can block true repentance.

He who heeds instruction and correction is [not only himself]
in the way of life [but also] is a way of life for others.
And he who neglects or refuses reproof [not only himself] goes
astray [but also] causes to err and is a path toward ruin for others.
Proverbs 10:17

When you do something wrong, do you try to change yourself? This is God's job. The amount of energy you spend trying — spend leaning.

When God shows us our faults,
to change we must trust, not try.

Doing the right thing with a wrong
attitude equals bad results.

The choices once made are our lives we now live.

If you want to sense God's direction for your life, you must give Him your destiny.

As for God, His way is perfect! The word of the Lord is tested and tried; He is a shield to all those who take refuge and put their trust in Him.

Psalm 18:30

Many have not learned to hear God's voice because they act in the flesh when not knowing what to do, instead of waiting on God.

In prayer, too many Christians wait
for the outcome to determine their attitude
when their attitude determines their outcome.

Being in the will of God is an attitude, not a place.

Negative situations are not permanent, so why should we allow our minds to be permanently ruled by them?

We often give our money to buy
the right to keep ourselves.

We can be carnal and go to heaven,
but we cannot be carnal and blessed on earth.

To be blessed with more, we must be blessed with what we have. To be blessed with what we have, we must be thankful.

When the devil knocks, let Jesus answer.

But to man He said, Behold, the reverential and worshipful fear of the Lord
— that is Wisdom; and to depart from evil is understanding.
Job 28:28

The devil cannot get a stronghold unless you give him a foothold.

Are you talking about the devil or to the devil when the pressure is on?

When you complain, you open the door for the devil and close the door to the answer.

Each offense committed against you becomes a brick by which you become walled in or wall the devil out, depending upon whether you show mercy or become bitter.

If you want to be blessed, learn to press through the test.

Blessed (happy, to be envied) is the man who is patient under trial and stands up under temptation, for when he has stood the test and been approved, he will receive [the victor's] crown of life which God has promised to those who love Him.

James 1:12

He who chooses the road that leads to reward will be accompanied by the companions of Obedience and Suffering.

For each person to move on to a higher level with God,
they must pass the test at the level they are.

The quality of commitment
is reflected in the cost.

Be constant, for both suffering and comfort are the same to a soul truly resigned to Him.

The prize in being a winner is found in the price of becoming a winner.

You must be willing to sacrifice, but not to compromise.

Success is the result of passing tests where we chose to do the best with the option to do less.

Faith is now, but the manifestation is in due time. So don't become impatient.

For you have need of steadfast patience and endurance, so that you may perform and fully accomplish the will of God, and thus receive and carry away [and enjoy to the full] what is promised.

Hebrews 10:36

The haste of man wastes the grace of God.

Waiting on the Lord is the action of faith.

Impatience is the fruit of the root of pride.

God is never in a hurry and never late because He has nowhere to go. He's already there.

Difficult situations are opportunities for God to do things to us or through us.

Consider it wholly joyful, my brethren, whenever you are enveloped in or encounter trials of any sort or fall into various temptations.

James 1:2

Christians must learn to maintain their joy in the midst of the storm, or the storm will remain.

Trials are gates to go through
on the road to success.

Situations do not cause stress.
Your reaction to situations causes stress.

Many people are trying to get to a place they enjoy instead of enjoying the place where they are.

If you don't learn how to deal with trouble,
trouble will deal with you.

Complaining keeps us nailed
to our problems.

God permits in His wisdom what He could have altered or prevented in His power.

To be able to love people when they are unlovely, we must learn to receive God's love when we have acted unlovely.

Fathers, do not provoke or irritate or fret your children [do not be hard on them or harass them], lest they become discouraged and sullen and morose and feel inferior and frustrated. [Do not break their spirit].

Colossians 3:21

The manifestation of pressure can produce aggravation which leads to frustration or reconciliation which leads to elevation — the choice is ours.

It's easy to be longsuffering with someone
if you have suffered long in the same areas.

Confrontation is a two-way street; no one has
the right-of-way unless they are willing to yield.

No one can properly confront another unless
he or she is willing to be confronted.

The beauty of Christianity is not the work we do,
but the relationship we maintain and the
atmosphere provided by that relationship.

A strong Christian is one who does the right thing under the wrong circumstances.

The Lord judges the people; judge me, O Lord, and do me justice according to my righteousness [my rightness, justice, and right standing with You] and according to the integrity that is in me.

Psalm 7:8

Mercy is our Father rescuing us out of distressful situations because of our relationship, not our record.

Some people are so afraid of failure
that they never succeed.

Focus on your capabilities instead of your flaws
if you don't want to be out of focus.

What you are is a result of what you've done where you've been.

When you start sinking, pay attention to what you're thinking.

Do not fret or have any anxiety about anything, but in every circumstance and in everything, by prayer and petition (definite requests), with thanksgiving, continue to make your wants known to God.

Philippians 4:6

Problems in our lives are not the cause of stress as much as our response to the problems.

A negative attitude that comes from trusting self will look at a situation that needs an answer and call it a problem.

A positive attitude that comes from trusting God will look at what others call a problem and call it a situation to which there is an answer.

One by fear focuses on the need;
the other by faith focuses on the answer.
Are you letting God be God or
trying to help God be God?

Nothing can be done through a Christian unless he has first allowed God to work humility in him.

Humility rejoices over those who have more and blesses those who have less.

Faith is an attitude of trust with humility,
not an attitude of assurance with pride.

A proud person tries to use God.
A humble person allows God to use him.

The Bible does not tell us to make the Word work. It tells us to let the Word work.

Moses told the people, Fear not; stand still (firm, confident, undismayed) and see the salvation of the Lord which He will work for you today. For the Egyptians you have seen today you shall never see again. The Lord will fight for you, and you shall hold your peace and remain at rest.

Exodus 14:13,14

Are you trying out God or are you sold out to God? The difference is faith instead of hope so.

Are you trying to do something about something that you can't do anything about? One thing is required: trust.

God is more interested in our stability than our tranquility.

Fear of tomorrow, today, will produce tomorrow what you fear today.

It's better to grow slow and solid than fast and fragile.

[Not in your own strength] for it is God Who is all the while effectually at work in you [energizing and creating in you the power and desire], both to will and to work for His good pleasure and satisfaction and delight.

Philippians 2:13

Each Christian is a vessel loaded with power and might, but few there are who have acquired the right to use this might due to a lack of obedience.

Responsibility is one's ability to respond
without being fond of what he is responsible for.

If you believe you won't succeed and don't, don't blame
someone else because you won't believe and don't.

The difference between discouragement and encouragement is determined by who we depend on, God or man.

Fear is a person believing he can
do nothing and neither can God.

Pride is a person believing he
can do anything without God.

Humility is a person believing he can do nothing but God can do all things.

The Bible teaches us to know who we are in Christ, not do we are in Christ.

Study and be eager and do your utmost to present yourself to God approved (tested by trial), a workman who has no cause to be ashamed, correctly analyzing and accurately dividing [rightly handling and skillfully teaching] the Word of Truth.

2 Timothy 2:15

Proper priorities produce peace.

To be content in the future, we must
learn the secret of being content now.

If you want to be led by the Spirit, don't hurry or worry.

And let the peace (soul harmony which comes) from Christ rule (act as umpire continually) in your hearts [deciding and settling with finality all questions that arise in your minds, in that peaceful state] to which as [members of Christ's] one body you were also called [to live]. And be thankful (appreciative), [giving praise to God always].

Colossians 3:15

When making a decision, after checking with your head, look into your heart. If you see peace, go ahead.

If we are going to walk in God's peace,
we must be willing to give Him our struggles.
For God has made us care-casters, not burden-bearers.

Peace is not peace unless it remains
in the midst of the storm.

If we will pray for people instead of trying to change them, we will save energy, see results and retain our peace.

Don't look for peace at the end of the storm.
Find it the midst, and you won't notice the storm.

Big messes are little messes ignored.

Dread is destroyed by doing without delay.

A child of God who has learned the joy of abandonment and lives in the peace of abandonment has the confidence that all things will work out to his good God's way.

When you learn to lean, God shows up on the scene.

Do not, therefore, fling away your fearless confidence, for it carries a great and glorious compensation of reward.

Hebrews 10:35

Are you dependent on God or independent of God?
Whichever you choose will determine your mood.

In any negative situation, I cannot be depressed if I am not
oppressed. I cannot be oppressed if I am not impressed.
Therefore, if I am not impressed, I remain at rest.

Determination is an attitude, not a feeling.
We must decide, not wait to be moved.

Determination opens the door for
extermination of procrastination.

You cannot stand still or you will stagnate; you must grow on with the Lord. This means you will need to grow up if you want to go on.

You don't have victory if you don't have problems;
you have victory if your problems don't have you.

We don't know what tomorrow holds,
but we do know that God holds tomorrow.

Satan wants us to be active in things we can't do anything about and passive in things we can do something about.

If you want to stabilize, you must be willing to sacrifice, but not to compromise.

To have balance is to maintain stability between two extremes.

Believers are not to follow after signs. Signs are to follow believers!

Good thoughts must be chosen;
they won't just fall into your mind.

A negative thought is a dose of death.

Many people can't receive forgiveness because they're too busy trying to achieve forgiveness.

Forgiveness is the fragrance the violet
sheds on the heel that crushed it.

To receive forgiveness, we must be able
to separate what we do from who we are.

When wrong becomes right, the conscience has lost its light.

Hope for what you want,
but pray for what God wants.

Pride compares itself with someone who has less;
self-pity compares itself with someone who has more.

If you are trapped by memories
of the past or bound by fears
of the future, you will not enjoy today.

If you will submit yourself to God, you will loose the Holy Ghost in your behalf.

Therefore humble yourselves [demote, lower yourselves in your own estimation] under the mighty hand of God, that in due time He may exalt you, Casting the whole of your care [all your anxieties, all your worries, all your concerns, once and for all] on Him, for He cares for you affectionately and cares about you watchfully.

1 Peter 5:6,7

Why do we get frustrated?
Because we are trying to be the Holy Spirit.

Having done all, enter the rest of God and let God do the rest.

For we who have believed (adhered to and trusted in and relied on God) do enter that rest, in accordance with His declaration that those [who did not believe] should not enter when He said, As I swore in My wrath, They shall not enter My rest; and this He said although [His] works had been completed and prepared [and waiting for all who would believe] from the foundation of the world.

Hebrews 4:3

If it's really faith, we will not struggle; we will enter God's rest and let Him deal with the trouble.

* * *

To contact the author write: Dave Meyer • Joyce Meyer Ministries
P. O. Box 655 • Fenton, Missouri 63026 • or call: (636) 349-0303

Internet Address: www.jmministries.org

Please include your prayer requests and comments when you write.

To contact the author in Canada, please write: Dave Meyer
Joyce Meyer Ministries Canada, Inc. • Lambeth Box 1300
London, ON N6P 1T5 • or call: (636) 349-0303

In Australia, please write: Dave Meyer
Joyce Meyer Ministries-Australia • Locked Bag 77
Mansfield Delivery Centre • Queensland 4122
or call: (07) 3349 1200

Additional copies of this book are available from your local bookstore.

Harrison House • Tulsa, Oklahoma 74153

Though Dave Meyer is seldom seen on the platform or heard on the radio, his position is key to the overall operation of Life In The Word, Inc./Joyce Meyer Ministries. As business administrator, Dave handles all the ministry's radio and television negotiations, finances, travel schedules, and product sales. Dave says, "I am called by God to be Joyce's covering, to get her to where God wants her to be. I make sure she does not get hurt, and I see to it that she does not get into trouble. God asked me to submit to the gift He put in my wife. He showed me that the gift was His and by submitting to the gift and allowing Joyce to do what God has called her to do, that I was submitting to Him."

Joyce says, "Dave is the greatest man I know. He is also the happiest, most content person I know. He enjoys life to the fullest. I believe, and so does he, that his joy is a result of submitting to God and not trying to be something that God was not calling him to be."

Both Dave and Joyce pray that this book will be a blessing to you as you apply the "nuggets" to the situations you face daily. The wisdom found in these truths provide Dave and Joyce with a constant source of encouragement, and they believe these nuggets will lift you up as well.

The Harrison House Vision Proclaiming the truth and the power
Of the Gospel of Jesus Christ with excellence;
Challenging Christians to live victoriously,
Grow spiritually, know God intimately.